CAN YOU FIND MY LOVE? ™

THINGS TO DO OUTSIDE

JAN MARQUART

www.CanYouFindMyLove.com

ISBN: 0967578051
ISBN-13: 9780967578057

Cover and Interior by Publish Pros
www.publishpros.com

Books currently available in the "Can You Find My Love?" Series

Seasons: Book1

Things To Do Outside: Book 2

Other Books by Jan Marquart

FOR ADULTS

Write to Heal

The Mindful Writer, Still the Mind, Free the Pen

The Basket Weaver, a Novel

Kate's Way, a Novel

Echoes from the Womb, a Book for Daughters

Voices from the Land

The Breath of Dawn, a Journey of Everyday Blessings

How to Write From Your Heart (booklet)

How to Write Your Own Memoir (booklet)

A Manual on How to Deal With a Bully in the Workplace

Cracked Open, a Book of Poems

A Writer's Wisdom

To:

_____

NAME

Thank you to all the parents, grandparents, teachers, doctors, daycare workers, and others who have supported my efforts.

Also, my appreciation to Rich Carnahan, who continues to help me publish this book series, and his son, Aiden, a special young man who has greatly influenced my work.

CAN YOU FIND MY LOVE?
was inspired by two little angels:
Landon James and Evelyn Kirsten.

Their proud parents are my sweet nephew, David
Maravel, and his beautiful wife, Shawn Maravel.

You have received this book
because someone loves you.

Look closely—you will find love hidden
in everyday things that you might
normally take for granted.

This is what it looks like.

♥

When you find the love I have placed
for you, I hope that it warms your
heart and lets you know how
very special you are.

Things To Do OUTSIDE

WATCH THE CLOUDS

Clouds shade us from the hot sun and
sometimes look like shapes we know.

JUMP ROPE

Flip the rope over your head and jump it when
it passes under your feet.

CAN YOU FIND MY LOVE?

SKIP

Skipping is in between walking, hopping and running. It is fun to skip with friends.

CAN YOU FIND MY LOVE?

FLY A KITE

Kites are powered by wind. Running into the wind will help your kite fly high into the air.

CAN YOU FIND MY LOVE?

PLAY LEAP FROG

Frogs jump over one another to catch flies for dinner. Kids can leap over one another too!

CAN YOU FIND MY LOVE?

RUN

Running is good exercise.
Line up with your friends and see who can
run the fastest. Ready...set...go!

CAN YOU FIND MY LOVE?

PLAY IN A SPRINKLER

It's hot in summer. Running through the spray from a hose or sprinkler will cool you off.

SWING

Swinging is a way to fly through the air
with no effort at all.

CAN YOU FIND MY LOVE?

GO TO THE PLAYGROUND

Playgrounds usually have swings, sandboxes, slides and merry-go-rounds to play on.

BUILD SANDCASTLES

Sandcastles can be made using sand, water and your hands, but you can also use buckets, spoons and shovels.

SWIM

Paddle your arms and kick your legs.
It's fun to glide through the water.

RIDE A BIKE

Get your bike moving fast by pushing down
on the pedals with your feet one at a time.

CAN YOU FIND MY LOVE?

WATCH THE STARS

Stars come out when the sun sets
and the sky gets dark. Try counting them.

CAN YOU FIND MY LOVE?

PLAY TAG

Tag is a game where one kid chases other
kids until someone gets caught.
If you're caught, you're "it."

PLAY A SPORT

Baseball, kickball, soccer and basketball are
just a few of the sports you can play outside
on a nice day.

CAN YOU FIND MY LOVE?

DIG FOR WORMS

Worms are found under the dirt, and their poop feeds the soil your plants grow in.

BUILD A SNOWMAN

Pack snow into large round balls, pile them on
top of one another and decorate them.

CAN YOU FIND MY LOVE?

GO FOR A WALK

Walking is great exercise. You'll
see things you don't get to see while
riding in a car.

RIDE A SCOOTER

Scooters are easy to ride. Use your foot to keep moving by pushing it along the ground.

ROLLER SKATE

Roller skates are like shoes with wheels.
You can skate alone or with your friends.

PLAY HOPSCOTCH

Draw numbered squares on the ground with chalk. Then toss a stone onto a number and hop over to pick it up.

PLAY IN THE RAIN

Rain is water that falls from the clouds.
It feels cool on our faces and
waters the plants.

GO FISHING

You can fish in lakes, ponds, rivers and the ocean using worms, peanut butter, bread or cheese as bait.

hAVE A PICNIC

Pack your favorite foods into a basket
and take them outside to eat on a blanket.

PLANT A GARDEN

Planting flowers, fruits and vegetables
lets you see how they grow.

Did you look close enough
to find all my love?

Can you **DRAW** a few other things you do **OUTSIDE**?

From:

_____

NAME

About the Author

Jan Marquart is a psychotherapist and author. She has published 11 books and has had articles, stories, poems, and essays published in various newspapers, journals, and magazines across the United States, Australia, and Europe. She teaches writing for those over fifty, and has taught a dozen writing workshops for Story Circle Network.

Jan has designed a 6-week writing course titled *Unveil the Wounded Self - Write to Heal* which focuses on healing PTSD and has also designed a 6-week writing course titled *The Provocation of Journal Writing* to encourage everyone to write their personal stories. She is currently on her 99th daily journal.

Jan can be contacted at JanMarquart.com, JanMarquartlcsw.wordpress.com and at her personal email address, jan_marquart@yahoo.com.

Her books can be purchased from all major online book retailers.

www.ingramcontent.com/pod-product-compliance
Lightning Source LLC
Chambersburg PA
CBHW040247100426
42811CB00011B/1183